THE VERY EMOTIONAL ANIMAL ALPHABET

AN ABC BOOK ABOUT AN ABC BOOK (AND SO MUCH MORE)

Written by Renee Jain
Illustrated by Rebecca Bagley

Dedicated to Jasmin and Jude,
the two magical beings who have opened
a new dimension of lightness and love in our lives.

Author: Renee Jain
Illustrator: Rebecca Bagley
Typographic Designer: Nikki Abramowitz

www.GoZen.com

ISBN: 1514302950
ISBN-13: 978-1-5143-0295-8

Alex the angry alligator is having one of his tantrums.

He is supposed to be learning his ABCs, but he threw his favorite alphabet book out of the open window – only to be caught by...

Barbara the baffled buffalo.

A book suddenly landing in her lap makes her even more baffled. Confused, Barbara bundles the book over to...

Bb

cathy the curious camel.

Being curious, Cathy flips through the book and sees that it belongs to someone called Alex.

"Do you know an Alex?" she asks, throwing the book to...

ABC

Cc

Danny the doubtful dragonfly.

"Erm, I'm not sure!" says Danny, doubtfully. "What should I do?" Danny turns to ask...

Dd

Ella the excited elephant.

"Yippee, yay, give it to me!"

The ground shakes as Ella jumps around. She reaches for the book with her trunk, but in the excitement it flies through the air, landing on...

Frank the frightened flamingo.

"Ahhhhh!" As Frank flaps around fitfully in fear, the alphabet book soars through the air once again, landing in the pond with...

Gg

Glen the grumpy goldfish.

"Get that out of here," Glen grunts grumpily. "Don't blame me when it's all soggy and ruined." Luckily...

Hh

Helen the happy heron
spies the book at her feet.

"Wow, a book! That's great,"
she says, smiling happily.

She plucks the soggy
book from the pond with
her beak and gives it to...

Ian the impatient iguana, to dry in the sun.

"This is NEVER going to dry," he says,
prodding at it impatiently. "Now look...
the ink is running," says Ian, tossing it up.

Right away, the book is snatched by...

Janet the jealous jackal.

"I want the alphabet book," she whines. "It's not Alex's, it's mine!"

Janet clamps the soggy book in her toothy jaws, until...

Kayla the kind kangaroo hops over for a chat.

"I really think it would be nice to get this book back to Alex, its actual owner," says Kayla kindly. She gently takes the book and hands it to...

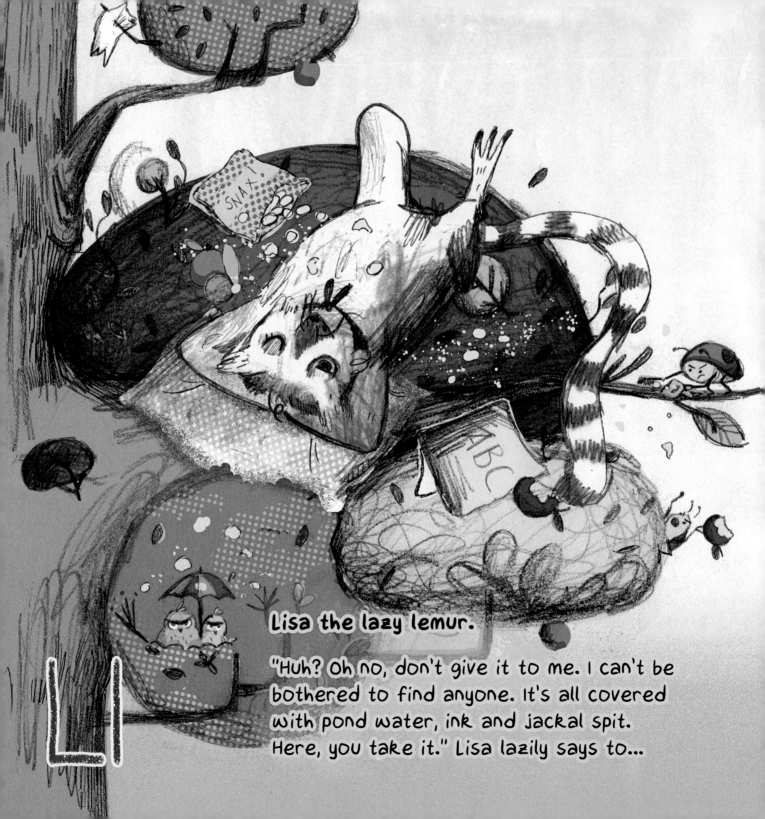

Lisa the lazy lemur.

"Huh? Oh no, don't give it to me. I can't be bothered to find anyone. It's all covered with pond water, ink and jackal spit. Here, you take it." Lisa lazily says to...

Ll

Matthew the mellow monkey.

"Oh, that's cool. Hey, It's a bit damp and tatty now, but I bet this Alex dude would still like it back. What do you think?" asks Matthew as he passes it to...

Mm

Nn

Norma the negative newt.

"Waste of time," says Norma negatively. "You'll never find this 'Alex' and even if you do, the book's ruined. See?" says Norma, nudging it near...

Ola the optimistic oyster.

"Oh, what a wonderful thing this is! I think it will clean up well. Can you help?" she asks as she passes it to...

Percy the panicky penguin.

"Eek, aah!" Percy panics and flaps about.
"This book is making me so nervous. Oh no..."
In his panic, he drops it into his fish bucket.

"Yuck!" says...

Pp

Quince the queasy quail, gagging and holding his nose as he plucks the book from Percy's lunch.

"Someone take it... I think I'm gonna..." Quince dashes off, looking a little green, and leaves the book with...

Rr

Ruby the remorseful rattlesnake, who examines the rather ruined, smelly book.

"Did I have something to do with messing up this book? I'm so sorry," she sighs, while passing it on to...

Sam the scared skunk.

"Yikes! Stinky things spook me.
Oh no, I made a stinky on myself!"
Terrified, Sam slides the book to...

Tt

Tina the tearful tiger.

"wahhh." Tina bursts into tears
at the terrible sight and smell.
The pages are wet, the ink is
running, and it smells of skunk.

"It's not so bad," says...

Uu

Una the uneasy umbrella bird.

Una takes the book, but drops it immediately.

"On second thought, holding a ruined book makes me feel uncomfortable." She nudges it over to...

Vern the vexed vulture.

"This is really irritating. I don't want this rotten old book to read!"

He angrily tries to fly away but...

Ww

Wendy the willful warthog stops him.

"We need to return this. If you lost your book, you'd want it back. We can do this! We just have to put our minds to it."

Wendy taps the fish tank and...

Xx

Xena the xenial x-ray tetra looks up.

"Greetings, welcome, please come in," says Xena merrily. "Oh, Alex yes, I had him over for a visit last week. I know he likes the library," she says, pointing toward...

Yen the yearning yak.

"I've wanted so badly to do a good deed. I'd be happy to return Alex's book."

He starts off toward the library when...

Yy

Zack the zealous zebra squeals, "I'm coming too. This is fantastic!"

Zack grins, zipping over to everyone with zest. "Oh, look, there's Alex!"

"Grr, what did you do to my book?" Alex the angry alligator rages.

Holding it by one corner, he examines the crumpled, soggy, spitty, fishy, stinky alphabet book... and then he sees the crowd of hopeful faces that worked so hard to get it back to him.

"But you guys barely know me," he says, his face softening.

"I'm amazed! I'm Alex the amazed alligator!"

LIBRARY

Find more fun adventures at
www.GoZen.com/toddlers

Made in the USA
Middletown, DE
16 August 2015